THE GREAT OPERAS OF

Vincenzo Bellini

—

An Account of the Life and Work of this Distinguished
Composer, with Particular Attention to his Operas.

—

By
GUSTAV KOBBÉ

—

British Library Cataloguing-in-Publication Data
A catalogue record for this book is available from
the British Library

A History of The Theatre

'The Theatre' is a collaborative form of fine art that uses live performers to present the experience of a real or imagined event. The performers may communicate this experience to the audience through combinations of gesture, speech, song, music, and dance, with elements of art, stagecraft and set design used to enhance the physicality, presence and immediacy of the experience. The specific place of the performance is also named by the word 'theatre' – derived from the Ancient Greek word *théatron*, meaning 'a place for viewing', itself from *theáomai*, meaning 'to see', 'watch' or 'observe'.

Modern Western theatre largely derives from ancient Greek drama, from which it borrows technical terminology, classification into genres, and many of its themes, stock characters, and plot elements. The city-state of Athens is where 'theatre' as we know it originated, as part of a broader culture of theatricality and performance in classical Greece that included festivals, religious rituals, politics, law, athletics, music, poetry, weddings, funerals, and symposia. Participation in the city-state's many festivals – and attendance at the City Dionysia as an audience member (or even as a participant in the theatrical productions) in particular, was an important part of citizenship.

The theatre of ancient Greece consisted of three types of drama: tragedy, comedy, and the satyr play (a form of tragicomedy, similar in spirit to the bawdy satire of burlesque). The origins of theatre in ancient Greece, according to Aristotle (384–322 BCE), the first theoretician of theatre, are to be found in the festivals that honoured Dionysus. These performances (the aforementioned City Dionysia) were held in semi-circular auditoria cut into hillsides, capable of seating 10,000–20,000 people. The stage consisted of a dancing floor (orchestra), dressing room and scene-building area (skene). Since the words were the most important part, good acoustics and clear delivery were paramount. The actors (always men) wore masks appropriate to the characters they represented, and each might play several parts.

Athenian tragedy (the oldest surviving form of tragedy) emerged sometime during the sixth century BCE, and flowered during the fifth century BCE – from the end of which it began to spread throughout the Greek world – and continued in popularity until the beginning of the Hellenistic period. Aeschylus, Sophocles, and Euripides were masters of the genre. The other side of the coin – Athenian comedy, is conventionally divided into three periods; 'Old Comedy', 'Middle Comedy', and 'New Comedy'. Old Comedy survives today largely in the form of the eleven surviving plays of Aristophanes, while Middle Comedy is largely lost (preserved only in a few relatively short fragments in authors such as Athenaeus of Naucratis). New Comedy is known primarily from the substantial papyrus fragments of Menander.

Western theatre developed and expanded considerably under the Romans. The theatre of ancient Rome was a thriving and diverse art form, ranging from festival performances of street theatre, nude dancing, and acrobatics, to the staging of Plautus's broadly appealing situation comedies, to the high-style, verbally elaborate tragedies of Seneca. Although Rome had a native tradition of performance, the Hellenization of Roman culture in the third century BCE had a profound and energizing effect on Roman theatre and encouraged the development of Latin literature of the highest quality for the stage. This tradition fed into the modern theatre we know today, and during the renaissance, theatre generally moved away from the poetic drama of the Greeks, and towards a more naturalistic prose style of dialogue. By the nineteenth century and the Industrial Revolution, this trend continued to progress.

In England, theatre was immensely popular, but took a big pause during 1642 and 1660 because of Cromwell's Interregnum. Prior to this, 'English renaissance theatre' was witnessed, with celebrated playwrights such as William Shakespeare, Christopher Marlowe and Ben Jonson. Under Queen Elizabeth, drama was a unified expression as far as social class was concerned, and the Court watched the same plays the commoners saw in the public playhouses. With the development of the private theatres, drama became more oriented towards the tastes and values of an upper-class audience however. By the later part of the reign of Charles I, few new plays were being written for the public theatres, which sustained themselves on the accumulated works of the previous decades. Theatre was now seen as something sinful and the Puritans tried very hard to drive it out of their society. Due to this stagnant period, once Charles II came back to the throne in 1660, theatre (among other arts) exploded with influences from France, and the wider continent.

The eighteenth century saw the widespread introduction of women to the stage – a development previously unthinkable. These women were looked at as celebrities (also a newer concept, thanks to ideas on individualism that were beginning to be born in Renaissance Humanism) but on the other hand, it was still very new and revolutionary. Comedies were full of the young and very much in vogue, with the storyline following their love lives: commonly a young roguish hero professing his love to the chaste and free minded heroine near the end of the play, much like Sheridan's *The School for Scandal.* Many of the comedies were fashioned after the French tradition, mainly Molière (the great comedic playwright), again harking back to the French influence of the King and his court after their exile.

After this point, there was an explosion of theatrical styles. Throughout the nineteenth century, the popular theatrical forms of Romanticism, melodrama, Victorian burlesque and the well-made plays of Scribe and Sardou gave way to the problem plays of Naturalism and Realism; the farces of Feydeau; Wagner's operatic *Gesamtkunstwerk*; musical theatre (including Gilbert and Sullivan's operas); F. C. Burnand's, W. S. Gilbert's and Wilde's drawing-room comedies; Symbolism; proto-Expressionism in the late works of August Strindberg and Henrik Ibsen; and Edwardian musical comedy. The list continues! These trends continued through the twentieth century in the realism of Stanislavski and Lee Strasberg, the political theatre of Erwin Piscator and Bertolt Brecht, the so-called Theatre of the Absurd of Samuel Beckett and Eugène Ionesco, and the rise of American and British musicals.

Theatre itself has an incredibly long history, and despite the massive proliferation of theatrical styles and mediums – it essentially owes its existence to the ancient Greeks and the Romans. The three main genres; tragedy, comedy and satyre, continue to influence plot themes, directing, writing and acting, with frequent and fascinating interrelations and overlaps. As a genre, it remains as popular today as it has ever been, and continues as a massive influence on popular culture more broadly. It is hoped that the current reader enjoys this book on the subject.

Vincenzo Bellini

(1802–1835)

BELLINI, born in Catania, Sicily, November 3, 1802, is the composer of "La Sonnambula," one of the most popular works of the old type of Italian opera still found in the repertoire. "I Puritani," another work by him, was given for the opening of two New York opera houses, Palmo's in 1844, and Hammerstein's Manhattan, in 1903. But it maintains itself only precariously. "Norma" is given still more rarely, although it contains "Casta diva," one of the most famous solos for soprano in the entire Italian repertory.

This composer died at the village of Puteaux, France, September 23, 1835, soon after the highly successful production of "I Puritani" in Paris, and while he was working on a commission to compose two operas for the San Carlo Theatre, Naples, which had come to him through the success of "Puritani." He was only thirty-two.

It is not unlikely that had this composer, with his facile and graceful gift for melody, lived longer he would have developed, as Verdi did, a maturer and broader style, and especially have paid more attention to the instrumentation of his operas, a detail which he sadly neglected.

LA SONNAMBULA

THE SLEEPWALKER

Opera in three acts by Bellini, words by Felice Romani. Produced, Carcano Theatre, Milan, March 6, 1831. London, King's Theatre,

Vincenzo Bellini

July 28, 1831; in English, Drury Lane, May 1, 1833. New York, Park Theatre, November 13, 1835, in English, with Brough, Richings, and Mr. and Mrs. Wood; in Italian, Palmo's Opera House, May 11, 1844; frequently sung by Gerster and by Adelina Patti at the Academy of Music, and at the Metropolitan Opera House by Sembrich; at the Manhattan Opera House by Tetrazzini.

CHARACTERS

COUNT RODOLPHO, Lord of the castle.............. *Bass*
TERESA, proprietress of the mill................... *Soprano*
AMINA, her foster daughter....................... *Soprano*
LISA, proprietress of the village inn................ *Soprano*
ELVINO, a young farmer.......................... *Tenor*
ALESSIO, a villager.............................. *Bass*
Notary, Villagers, etc.
Time—Early Nineteenth Century.   *Place*—A Village in Switzerland.

Act I.   The village green.   On one side an inn.   In the background a water mill.   In the distance mountains.   As the curtain rises the villagers are making merry, for they are about to celebrate a nuptial contract between *Amina*, an orphan brought up as the foster child of *Teresa*, the mistress of the village mill, and *Elvino*, a young landowner of the neighbourhood.   These preparations, however, fill with jealousy the heart of *Lisa*, the proprietress of the inn.   For she is in love with *Elvino*.   Nor do *Alessio's* ill-timed attentions please her.   *Amina* enters under the care of *Teresa*, and returns her thanks to her neighbours for their good wishes.   She has two attractive solos.   These are "Come per me sereno" (How, for me brightly shining)

and "Sovia il sen la man mi posa" (With this heart its joy revealing).

2

Both are replete with grace and charm.

When the village *Notary* and *Elvino* appear the contract is signed and attested, and *Elvino* places a ring on *Amina's* finger. Duet: "Prendi l'avel ta dono" (Take now the ring I give you), a composition in long-flowing expressive measures.

Then the village is startled by the crack of whips and the rumble of wheels. A handsome stranger in officer's fatigue uniform appears. He desires to have his horses watered and fed, before he proceeds to the castle. The road is bad, night is approaching. Counselled by the villagers, and urged by *Lisa*, the officer consents to remain the night at the inn.

The villagers know it not at this time, but the officer is *Rodolpho*, the lord of the castle. He looks about him and recalls the scenes of his youth: "Vi ravviso" (As I view).

He then gallantly addresses himself to *Amina* in the charming air, "Tu non sai in quel begli occhi" (You know not, maid, the light your eyes within).

Elvino is piqued at the stranger's attentions to his bride, but *Teresa* warns all present to retire, for the village is said to be haunted by a phantom. The stranger treats the superstition lightly, and, ushered in by *Lisa*, retires to the village inn. All then wend their several ways homeward. *Elvino*, however, finds time to upbraid *Amina* for seemingly having found much pleasure in the stranger's gallant speeches, but before they part there are mutual concessions and forgiveness.

Act II. *Rodolpho's* sleeping apartment at the inn. He enters, conducted by *Lisa*. She is coquettish, he quite willing to meet her halfway in taking liberties with her. He learns from her that his identity as the lord of the castle has now been discovered by the villagers, and that they will shortly come to the inn to offer their congratulations. He is annoyed, but quite willing that *Lisa's* attractions shall atone therefor. At that moment, however, there is a noise without, and *Lisa* escapes into an adjoining room. In her haste she drops her handkerchief, which *Rodolpho* picks up and hangs over the bedpost. A few moments later he is amazed to see *Amina*, all in white, raise his window and enter his room. He realizes almost immediately that she is walking in her sleep, and that it is her somnambulism which has given rise to the superstition of the village phantom. In her sleep *Amina* speaks of her approaching marriage, of *Elvino's* jealousy, of their quarrel and reconciliation. *Rodolpho*, not wishing to embarrass her by his presence should she suddenly awaken, extinguishes the candles, steps out of the window and closes it lightly after him. Still asleep *Amina* sinks down upon the bed.

The villagers enter to greet *Rodolpho*. As the room is darkened, and, to their amusement, they see the figure of a woman on the bed, they are about to withdraw discreetly, when *Lisa*, who knows what has happened, enters with a light, brings in *Elvino*, and points out *Amina* to him. The light, the sounds, awaken her. Her natural confusion at the situation in which she finds herself is mistaken by *Elvino* for evidence of guilt. He casts her off. The others, save *Teresa*, share his suspicions. *Teresa*, in a simple, natural

21

way, takes the handkerchief hanging over the bedpost and places it around *Amina's* neck, and when the poor, grief-stricken girl swoons, as *Elvino* turns away from her, her foster-mother catches her in her arms.

In this scene, indeed in this act, the most striking musical number is the duet near the end. It is feelingly composed, and, as befits the situation of a girl mistakenly, yet none the less cruelly, accused by her lover, is almost wholly devoid of vocal embellishment. It begins with *Amina's* protestations of innocence: "D'un pensiero, et d'un accento" (Not in thought's remotest region).

When *Elvino's* voice joins hers there is no comfort for her in his words. He is still haunted by dark suspicions.

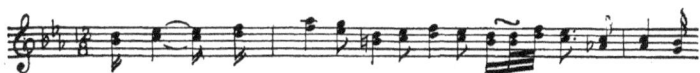

An unusual and beautiful effect is the closing of the duet with an expressive phrase for tenor alone: "Questo pianto del mio cor" (With what grief my heart is torn).

Act III, Scene 1. A shady valley between the village and the castle. The villagers are proceeding to the castle to beg *Rodolpho* to intercede with *Elvino* for *Amina*. *Elvino* meets *Amina*. Still enraged at what he considers her perfidy, he snatches from her finger the ring he gave her. *Amina* still loves him. She expresses her feelings in the air: "Ah! perche non posso odiarti" (Ah! Why is it I cannot hate him).

Scene 2. The village, near *Teresa's* mill. Water runs through the race and the wheel turns rapidly. A slender wooden bridge, spanning the wheel, gives access from some dormer lights in the millroof to an old stone flight of steps leading down to the foreground.

Lisa has been making hay while the sun shines. She has induced *Elvino* to promise to marry her. Preparations for the wedding are on foot. The villagers have assembled. *Rodolpho* endeavours to dissuade *Elvino* from the step he is about to take. He explains that *Amina* is a somnambulist. But *Elvino* has never heard of somnambulism. He remains utterly incredulous.

Teresa begs the villagers to make less disturbance, as poor *Amina* is asleep in the mill. The girl's foster-mother learns of *Elvino's* intention of marrying *Lisa*. Straightway she takes from her bosom *Lisa's* handkerchief, which she found hanging over *Rodolpho's* bedpost. *Lisa* is confused. *Elvino* feels that she, too, has betrayed him. *Rodolpho* again urges upon *Elvino* that *Amina* never was false to him— that she is the innocent victim of sleepwalking.

"Who can prove it?" *Elvino* asks in agonized tones.

"Who? She herself!—See there!" exclaims *Rodolpho*.

For at that very moment *Amina*, in her nightdress, lamp in hand, emerges from a window in the mill roof. She passes along, still asleep, to the lightly built bridge spanning the mill wheel, which is still turning round quickly. Now she sets foot on the narrow, insecure bridge. The villagers fall on their knees in prayer that she may cross safely. *Rodolpho* stands among them, head uncovered. As *Amina* crosses the bridge a rotting plank breaks under her footsteps. The lamp falls from her hand into the torrent beneath. She, however, reaches the other side, and gains the stone steps, which she descends. Still walking in her sleep, she advances to where stand the villagers and *Rodolpho*. She kneels and prays for *Elvino*. Then rising, she speaks of the ring he has taken from her, and draws from her bosom the flowers given to her by him on the previous day. "Ah! non credea mirarti, si presto estinto o flore" (Scarcely could I believe it that so soon thou would'st wither, O blossoms).

Gently *Elvino* replaces the ring upon her finger, and kneels before her. "Viva Amina!" cry the villagers. She awakens. Instead of sorrow, she sees joy all around her, and *Elvino*, with arms outstretched, waiting to beg her forgiveness and lead her to the altar.

> "Ah! non giunge uman pensiero
> Al contento ond' io son piena"
> (Mingle not an earthly sorrow
> With the rapture now o'er me stealing).

It ends with this brilliant passage:

The "Ah! non giunge" is one of the show pieces of Italian opera. Nor is its brilliance hard and glittering. It is the brightness of a tender soul rejoicing at being enabled to cast off sorrow. Indeed, there is about the entire opera a sweetness and a gentle charm, that go far to account for its having endured so long in the repertoire, out of which so many works far more ambitious have been dropped.

Vincenzo Bellini

Opera-goers of the old Academy of Music days will recall the bell-like tones of Etelka Gerster's voice in "Ah! non giunge"; nor will they ever forget the bird-like, spontaneous singing in this rôle of Adelina Patti, gifted with a voice and an art such as those who had the privilege of hearing her in her prime have not heard since, nor are likely to hear again. Admirers of Mme. Sembrich's art also are justly numerous, and it is fortunate for habitués of the Metropolitan that she was so long in the company singing at that house. She was a charming *Amina*. Tetrazzini was brilliant in "La Sonnambula." *Elvino* is a stick of a rôle for tenor. *Rodolpho* has the redeeming grace of chivalry. *Amina* is gentle, charming, appealing.

The story of "Sonnambula" is simple and thoroughly intelligible, which cannot be said for all opera plots. The mainspring of the action is the interesting psycho-physical manifestation of somnambulism. This is effectively worked out. The crossing of the bridge in the last scene is a tense moment in the simple story. It calls for an interesting stage "property"—the plank that breaks without precipitating *Amina*, who sometimes may have more embonpoint than voice, into the mill-race. All these elements contribute to the success of "La Sonnambula," which, produced in 1831, still is a good evening's entertainment.

Amina was one of Jenny Lind's favourite rôles. There is a beautiful portrait of her in the character by Eichens. It shows her, in the last act, kneeling and singing "Ah! non credea," and is somewhat of a rarity. A copy of it is in the print department of the New York Public Library. It is far more interesting than her better known portraits.

NORMA

Opera in two acts, by Bellini; words by Felice Romani, based on an old French story. Produced, December 26, 1831, Milan. King's Theatre, June 20, 1833, in Italian; Drury Lane, June 24, 1837, in Eng-

The Complete Opera Book

lish. Paris, Théâtre des Italiens, 1833. New York, February 25, 1841, at the Park Theatre; October 2, 1854, for the opening of the Academy of Music, with Grisi, Mario, and Susini; December 19, 1891, Metropolitan Opera House, with Lilli Lehmann as *Norma*.

CHARACTERS

POLLIONE, Roman Pro-consul in Gaul......................*Tenor*
OROVESO, Archdruid, father of Norma.....................*Bass*
NORMA, High-priestess of the druidical temple of Esus.......*Soprano*
ADALGISA, a virgin of the temple........................*Contralto*
CLOTILDA, Norma's confidante...........................*Soprano*
FLAVIUS, a centurion...................................*Tenor*
Priests, Officers of the Temple, Gallic Warriors, Priestesses and Virgins
of the Temple, and Two Children of Norma and Pollione.
Time—Roman Occupation, about 50 B.C.   *Place*—Gaul.

Act I. Sacred grove of the Druids. The high priest *Oroveso* comes with the Druids to the sacred grove to beg of the gods to rouse the people to war and aid them to accomplish the destruction of the Romans. Scarcely have they gone than the Roman Pro-consul *Pollione* appears and confides to his Centurion, *Flavius*, that he no longer loves *Norma*, although she has broken her vows of chastity for him and has borne him two sons. He has seen *Adalgisa* and loves her.

At the sound of the sacred instrument of bronze that calls the Druids to the temple, the Romans disappear. The priests and priestesses approach the altar. *Norma*, the high priestess, daughter of *Oroveso*, ascends the steps of the altar. No one suspects her intimacy with the Roman enemy. But she loves the faithless man and therefore seeks to avert the danger that threatens him, should Gaul rise against the Romans, by prophesying that Rome will fall through its own weakness, and declaring that it is not yet the will of the gods that Gaul shall go to war. She also prays to the "chaste goddess" for the return of the Roman leader, who

9

Vincenzo Bellini

has left her. Another priestess is kneeling in deep prayer. This is *Adalgisa*, who also loves *Pollione*.

The scene changes and shows *Norma's* dwelling. The priestess is steeped in deep sadness, for she knows that *Pollione* plans to desert her and their offspring, although she is not yet aware of her rival's identity. *Adalgisa* comes to her to unburden her heart to her superior. She confesses that to her faith she has become untrue through love—and love for a Roman. *Norma*, thinking of her own unfaithfulness to her vows, is about to free *Adalgisa* from hers, when *Pollione* appears. Now she learns who the beloved Roman of *Adalgisa* is. But the latter turns from *Pollione*. She loves *Norma* too well to go away with the betrayer of the high-priestess.

Act II. *Norma*, filled with despair, is beside the cradle of her little ones. An impulse to kill them comes over her. But motherhood triumphs over unrequited love. She will renounce her lover. *Adalgisa* shall become the happy spouse of *Pollione*, but shall promise to take the place of mother to her children. *Adalgisa*, however, will not hear of treachery to *Norma*. She goes to *Pollione*, but only to remind him of his duty.

The scene changes again to a wooded region of the temple in which the warriors of Gaul have gathered. *Norma* awaits the result of *Adalgisa's* plea to *Pollione;* then learns that she has failed and has come back to the grove to pass her life as a priestess. *Norma's* wrath is now beyond control. Three times she strikes the brazen shield; and, when the warriors have gathered, they joyfully hear her message: War against the Romans! But with their deep war song now mingles the sound of tumult from the temple. A Roman has broken into the sacred edifice. He has been captured. It is *Pollione*, who she knows has sought to carry off *Adalgisa*. The penalty for his intrusion is death. But *Norma*, moved by love to pity, and still hoping to save her

recreant lover, submits a new victim to the enraged Gauls—
a perjured virgin of the priesthood.

"Speak, then, and name her!" they cry.

To their amazement she utters her own name, then
confesses all to her father, and to his care confides her
children.

A pyre has been erected. She mounts it, but not alone.
Pollione, his love rekindled at the spectacle of her greatness
of soul, joins her. In the flames he, too, will atone for their
offences before God.

The ambition of every dramatic soprano of old was to
don the robes of a priestess, bind her brow with the mystic
vervain, take in her hand a golden sickle, and appear in the
sacred grove of the Druids, there to invoke the chaste
goddess of the moon in the famous "Casta diva." Prima
donnas of a later period found further inspiration thereto
in the beautiful portrait of Grisi as *Norma*. Perhaps the
last to yield to the temptation was Lilli Lehmann, who, not
content with having demonstrated her greatness as *Brünn-
hilde* and *Isolde*, desired in 1891, to demonstrate that she
was also a great *Norma* a demonstration which did not
cause her audience to become unduly demonstrative. The
fact is, it would be difficult to revive successfully "Norma"
as a whole, although there is not the slightest doubt that
"Casta diva, che in argenti" (Chaste goddess, may thy silver
beam), is one of the most exquisite gems of Italian song.

It is followed immediately by "Ah! bello a me ritorna"
(Beloved, return unto me), which, being an allegro, con-
trasts effectively with the long, flowing measures of "Casta
diva."

Vincenzo Bellini

Before this in the opera there has occurred another familiar number, the opening march and chorus of the Druids, "Dell' aura tua profetica" (With thy prophetic oracle).

There is a fine trio for *Norma*, *Adalgisa*, and *Pollione*, at the end of the first act, "Oh! di qual sci tu vittima" (O, how his art deceived you).

In the scene between *Norma*, and *Adalgisa*, in the second act, is the duet, "Mira, O, Norma!" (Hear me, Norma)

Among the melodious passages in the opera, this is second in beauty only to "Casta diva."

I PURITANI

THE PURITANS

Opera in three acts, by Bellini; words by Count Pepoli. Produced, Paris, Théâtre des Italiens, January 25, 1835, with Grisi as *Elvira*, Rubini as *Arturo*, Tamburini as *Riccardo* and Lablanche as *Giorgio*. London, King's Theatre, May 21, 1835, in Italian (I Puritani ed i Cavaliere). New York, February 3, 1844; Academy of Music, 1883, with Gerster; Manhattan Opera House, December 3, 1906, with Bonci as *Arturo*, and Pinkert as *Elvira;* and in 1909 with Tetrazzini as *Elvira.*

CHARACTERS

LORD GAUTIER WALTON of the Puritans....................*Bass*
SIR GEORGE WALTON, his brother, of the Puritans...........*Bass*

The Complete Opera Book

LORD ARTHUR TALBOT, of the Cavaliers.....................*Tenor*
SIR RICHARD FORTH, of the Puritans.......................*Baritone*
SIR BENNO ROBERTSON, of the Puritans....................*Tenor*
HENRIETTA, of France, widow of Charles I.................*Soprano*
ELVIRA, daughter of Lord Walton..........................*Soprano*
Puritan , Soldiers of the Commonwealth, Men-at-Arms, Women, Pages, etc.
Time—During the Wars between Cromwell and the Stuarts.
Place—Near Plymouth, England.

Act I is laid in a fortress near Plymouth, held by *Lord Walton* for Cromwell. *Lord Walton's* daughter, *Elvira*, is in love with *Lord Arthur Talbot*, a cavalier and adherent of the Stuarts, but her father has promised her hand to *Sir Richard Forth*, like himself a follower of Cromwell. He relents, however, and *Elvira* is bidden by her uncle, *Sir George Walton*, to prepare for her nuptials with *Arthur*, for whom a safe conduct to the fortress has been provided.

Queen Henrietta, widow of Charles I., is a prisoner in the fortress. On discovering that she is under sentence of death, *Arthur*, loyal to the Stuarts, enables her to escape by draping her in *Elvira's* bridal veil and conducting her past the guards, as if she were the bride. There is one critical moment. They are met by *Sir Richard*, who had hoped to marry *Elvira*. The men draw their swords, but a disarrangement of the veil shows *Sir Richard* that the woman he supposes to be *Lord Arthur's* bride is not *Elvira*. He permits them to pass. When the escape is discovered, *Elvira*, believing herself deserted, loses her reason. Those who had gathered for the nuptials, now, in a stirring chorus, invoke maledictions upon *Arthur's* head.

Act II plays in another part of the fortress. It concerns itself chiefly with the exhibition of *Elvira's* madness. But it has also the famous martial duet, "Suoni la tromba" (Sound the trumpet), in which *Sir George* and *Sir Richard* announce their readiness to meet *Arthur* in battle and strive to avenge *Elvira's* sad plight.

Vincenzo Bellini

Act III is laid in a grove near the fortress. *Arthur*, although proscribed, seeks out *Elvira*. Her joy at seeing him again, temporarily lifts the clouds from her mind, but renewed evidence of her disturbed mental state alarms her lover. He hears men, whom he knows to be in pursuit of him, approaching, and is aware that capture means death, but he will not leave *Elvira*. He is apprehended and is about to be executed when a messenger arrives with news of the defeat of the Stuarts and a pardon for all prisoners. *Arthur* is freed. The sudden shock of joy restores *Elvira's* reason. The lovers are united.

As an opera "I Puritani" lacks the naïveté of "La Sonnambula," nor has it any one number of the serene beauty of the "Casta diva" in "Norma." Occasionally, however, it is revived for a tenor like Bonci, whose elegance of phrasing finds exceptional opportunity in the rôle of *Arthur;* or for some renowned prima donna of the brilliant coloratura type, for whom *Elvira* is a grateful part.

The principal musical numbers are, in act first, *Sir Richard Forth's* cavatina, "Ah! per sempre io ti perdei" (Ah! forever have I lost thee); *Arthur's* romance, "A te o cara (To thee, beloved);

A te o ca - ra,... a - mor ta- lo - ra,

and *Elvira's* sparkling polacca, "Son vergin vezzosa" (I am a blithesome maiden).

Son ver . . . gin vez . zo . . .   sa . in
ve . . , eta.   di'   spo . , . - sa,.

In the second act we have *Elvira's* mad scene, "Qui la voce sua soave" (It was here in sweetest accents)

For *Elvira* there also is in this act the beautiful air, "Vien, diletto" (Come, dearest love).

The act closes with the duet for baritone and bass, between *Sir Richard* and *Sir George*, "Suoni la tromba," a fine proclamation of martial ardour, which "in sonorousness, majesty and dramatic intensity," as Mr. Upton writes, "hardly has an equal in Italian opera."

"A una fonte afflitto e solo" (Sad and lonely by a fountain), a beautiful number for *Elvira* occurs in the third act.

There also is in this act the impassioned "Star teco ognor" (Still to abide), for *Arthur*, with *Elvira's* reply, "Caro, non ho parola" (All words, dear love are wanting).

It was in the duet at the end of Act II, on the occasion of the opera's revival for Gerster that I heard break and go to pieces the voice of Antonio Galassi, the great baritone of the heyday of Italian opera at the Academy of Music. "Suoni la tromba!"—He could sound it no more. The career of a great artist was at an end.

"I Puritani" usually is given in Italian, several of the characters having Italian equivalents for English names— *Arturo, Riccardo, Giorgio, Enrichetta*, etc.

The first performance in New York of "I Puritani," which opened Palmo's Opera House, was preceded by a "public rehearsal," which was attended by "a large audience composed of the Boards of Aldermen, editors,

Vincenzo Bellini

police officers, and musical people," etc. Signora Borghese and Signor Antognini "received vehement plaudits." Antognini, however, does not appear in the advertised cast of the opera. Signora Borghese was *Elvira*, Signor Perozzi *Arturo*, and Signor Valtellino *Giorgio*. The performance took place Friday, February 2, 1844.